THE REWRITTEN LIFE
LEADER GUIDE

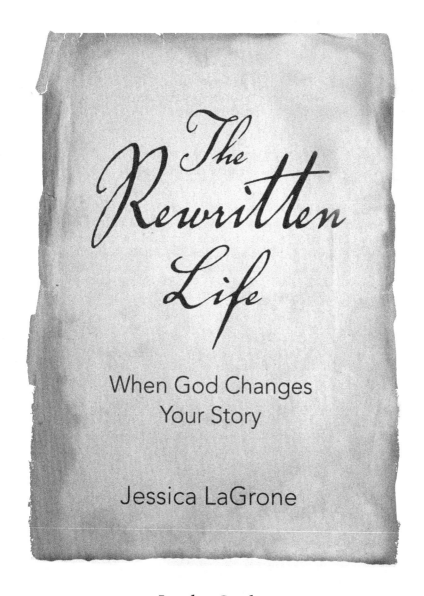

The
Rewritten
Life

When God Changes
Your Story

Jessica LaGrone

Leader Guide
by Jenny Youngman

Abingdon Press / Nashville

THE REWRITTEN LIFE
WHEN GOD CHANGES YOUR STORY
LEADER GUIDE

This book is printed on elemental chlorine-free paper.
ISBN 978-1-5018-3445-5

17 18 19 20 21 22 23 24 25 26 — 10 9 8 7 6 5 4 3 2 1
MANUFACTURED IN THE UNITED STATES OF AMERICA

CONTENTS

INTRODUCTION

Every name tells a story. In Scripture, God often changes individuals' names when God changes their stories. Changing someone's story involves transforming a life, bringing a new identity and a new journey. Today God changes our stories when we choose to follow and emerge as new creations in Christ.

The Rewritten Life: When God Changes Your Story is a study that explores God's transformational power through the stories of people in the Bible who encountered God and whose lives were never the same. Over the next six weeks, your group will explore the stories of Abraham and Sarah, Jacob, Naomi, Daniel, Peter, and an unnamed woman who was condemned by religious leaders before Jesus intervened. Together you will discover that God wants to be just as intimately involved in *your* stories, offering each of you an identity that shines with the purpose for which you were created—to know God through Jesus, God's Son, and to become more and more like him, bringing God glory.

In addition to discovering how God works to bring this transformation in our lives, you also will explore how God is revealed to us in Scripture—and how God desires to be known personally by each and every one of us. We serve a God who reveals and transforms. And we come to know God in deeper and more personal ways as we allow God to rewrite our stories.

About This Study

Before beginning this study, be sure that each participant has a copy of the book. Communicate to participants that they are to read the first chapter before the first session. Each week as you gather, you will have the opportunity to watch a 6-to7-minute video, discuss and reflect on Scripture, and pray together.

This book provides outlines for six group sessions, each formatted for a 60-minute session. Each session plan follows this format:

Bible Story Overview

For your preparation, this section provides a brief overview of the Bible story and the corresponding book chapter. Read this section before your meeting to refresh your memory and have an idea of where the conversation might be headed. Because not all participants will have read the corresponding chapter in the book, you might want to open each session by reading aloud this section.

Main Point

The Main Point summarizes the essential take-aways from the session and serves as a foundation for your discussion.

Key Scriptures

While you will need to have Bibles on hand during your session—and while you are encouraged to spend time in Bible study and reflection as you prepare to lead—each session includes the printed text of the key Scriptures. Use the Scriptures in your own preparation and/or read them aloud to the group as a part of each session.

What You Will Need

For each session, you will need *The Rewritten Life* DVD and a DVD player, a markerboard or chart paper, and markers.

Opening Prayer (3 minutes)

Open each week with prayer. Each session includes a printed prayer you may pray to begin your session.

Discussion Starter (5 minutes)

Use the ice-breaker question to get things started and to get people talking and comfortable in the group setting.

Video (7 minutes)

Following the opening and discussion starter, play the video segment on the DVD.

Video Discussion and Bible Study (30 minutes)

You will find that more discussion points and questions have been provided than you will have time to include. Before the session, select those you want to cover, and put a check mark beside them. As you discuss these questions, participants will need Bibles to look up supplementary Scriptures.

Deeper Conversation (10-15 minutes)

After your discussion, write on a markerboard or chart paper the week's deeper conversation question. Divide into smaller groups of two or three to discuss this question.

Closing Prayer (3 minutes)

Close each session by taking personal prayer requests from group members and leading the group in prayer. As you progress to later weeks in the study, you might encourage members to participate in the Closing Prayer by praying aloud for each other and the requests given.

BEFORE YOU BEGIN

While prayer and preparation are essential to a successful group study, you will get the most out of your time together if you modify each session to fit your teaching style, the needs and interests of your group, and your time constraints. Decide beforehand which elements of the session are most essential and which can be cut or altered for time. Anticipate questions or concerns that participants might raise with regard to a particular Scripture or discussion starter and consider how you will respond. Find other ways to take ownership of the study and make it fit your group. May God richly bless your time together as you study the Scriptures and discover the wonderful things that happen when God rewrites our stories!

Session 1

ABRAHAM AND SARAH

Bible Story Overview

God is actively participating in our stories, editing them or even rewriting them altogether. We see examples of this throughout Scripture, beginning in the opening chapters of the Book of Genesis and continuing throughout the closing pages of the New Testament.

Twelve chapters into Genesis we meet a couple named Abram and Sarai. God chose them specifically to be the parents of a great nation. There was one problem: When God made this promise to Abram and Sarai, they had no children and Abram was already seventy-five years old. Sarai was younger, but still well past child-bearing years. While God insisted that they would have a child and that their descendants would be numerous, their son would not be born for another twenty-five years.

When Abram was ninety-nine, and still childless, God gave him a new name, Abraham, meaning "ancestor of a multitude." Sarai became "Sarah," meaning princess. Giving these names to an elderly couple who'd spent more than two decades waiting on a promised child that still hadn't arrived was almost cruel. Shortly thereafter, when God sent a messenger to tell Abraham and Sarah that they'd have a child in one year, Sarah laughed. God even gave their son the name Isaac, which means, "He laughs."

At times, Abraham and Sarah struggled to remain faithful. (They even took matters into their own hands and arranged for Abraham to have a child, Ishmael, with Sarah's servant Hagar.) But they also grew in their relationship with God during their quarter century of waiting, and God continued working in their lives. When Isaac finally arrived, Abraham and Sarah had different names, different hearts, a different marriage, and a different outlook on God's promises.

Main Point

God's plans for us are beyond anything we ever dared to dream, but we may have to wait many years before these plans are realized. Though we wait, we can trust God because God is always faithful.

Key Scriptures

When Abram was ninety-nine years old, the Lord appeared to Abram, and said to him, "I am God Almighty; walk before me, and be blameless. And I will make my covenant between me and you, and will make you exceedingly numerous." Then Abram fell on his face; and God said to him, "As for me, this is my covenant with you: You shall be the ancestor of a multitude of nations. No longer shall your name be Abram, but your name shall be Abraham; for I have made you the ancestor of a multitude of nations. I will make you exceedingly fruitful; and I will make nations of you, and kings shall come from you. I will establish my covenant between me and you, and your offspring after you throughout their generations, for an everlasting covenant, to be God to you and to your offspring after you. And I will give to you, and to your offspring after you, the land where you are now an alien, all the land of Canaan, for a perpetual holding; and I will be their God."

(Genesis 17:1-8)

God said to Abraham, "As for Sarai your wife, you shall not call her Sarai, but Sarah shall be her name. I will bless her, and moreover I will give you a son by her. I will bless her, and she shall give rise to nations; kings of peoples shall come from her."

(Genesis 17:15-16)

Let us fix our eyes on Jesus, the author and perfecter of our faith.

(Hebrews 12:1b-2 NIV, 1984)

What You Will Need

- *The Rewritten Life* DVD and a DVD player
- Markerboard or chart paper and markers

SESSION OUTLINE

Opening Prayer (3 minutes)

Lead the following prayer or one of your own:

Dear God,

You know us so well. You know that we are one big mess of contradictions— hungering for change and resisting it at the same time. Change our hearts so that we willingly allow you to change us—to rewrite our stories and make us like your Son, Jesus Christ. Give us hearts like his; shape our identities so people will recognize his likeness in us. Begin to whisper to us the dreams you have for us—dreams far more wonderful than anything we could ever ask or imagine. Let us surrender, that you might transform us into the new creations we are meant to be. Prepare our hearts and minds now for all that you have for us today. In Jesus' name we pray. Amen.

Discussion Starter (5 minutes)

Use the following question as an icebreaker.

- If you were to describe your life story by bookstore categories, would you categorize your life as romance, action, thriller, historical fiction, or cookbook? Why?

Video (7 minutes)

Play the Session 1 video segment on the DVD.

Video Discussion and Bible Study (30 minutes)

More discussion points, questions, and Bible study questions have been provided than you will have time to include. Before the session, select those you want to cover, and put a check mark beside them.

1. Abram and Sarai were utterly transformed by the promise of God's blessings. Have three volunteers read aloud Genesis 12:1-3, Genesis 15:4-5, and Genesis 17:1-6, 15-16. Discuss:
   o What promises did God make to Abram and Sarai?
   o Why did God change their names, and what did their new names mean?
   o How do you think these name changes, and the promises of God they reflected, might have affected Abram and Sarai?

2. Abram and Sarai's story was shaping up to be a tragedy, not a fairy tale. But God is in the business of rewriting stories. God is not content to let our stories unfold without a word of God's love and grace marking us forever.
   o When have you sensed that God was rewriting some aspect of your story? How did your life change as a result?
   o In what ways did God rewrite Abram and Sarai's story?

3. God had plans for Abram and Sarai that were far beyond anything they dreamed of. Have two volunteers read aloud Jeremiah 29:11 and Ephesians 3:20.
   o What do these verses say about the plans God has for us?
   o How do you know what plans God has for your life?
   o When have God's plans for your life exceeded your imagination?

4. Have someone read aloud Genesis 17:1-8 and note how many times that God says, "I will."
   o How many times did you find "I will" in these verses?
   o Is this phrase in first, second, or third person?
   o Is this phrase in past, present, or future tense?
   o What conclusion can you draw based on these answers?

5. God is capable of fulfilling every promise God makes. God's promises to Abraham and Sarah—and to us—can be summarized with three words: people, place, and presence.
   o How do God's promises to Abraham and Sarah involve people?
   o How do God's promises to Abraham and Sarah involve place?

- o How do God's promises to Abraham and Sarah involve God's presence?
- o How has God brought blessings into your life in these three categories?

6. For Abraham and Sarah, trusting God's promises meant a lot of waiting. But, in waiting, they grew in their faith, trust, and hope in God. Often something powerful happens within us while we are waiting. When we wait, we are still long enough for God to do important work within us, molding us into the person God wants us to become. Waiting for God's blessing often is part of the blessing itself, since we have to rely on God in new and unexpected ways.

- o When have you found yourself waiting on God? How did this time of waiting result in blessing or growth?
- o What can we learn about God as we trust God in our waiting?
- o How has waiting changed you or your relationship with God?

7. True change is found in discovering who God is, how God and God's love are revealed to us, and how God makes a difference in our own lives. Only when we begin to see God's unchanging character do we find ourselves wanting to change to be more like God. God's name is a representation of God's character, promises, and strength. When we call on God's name, we are asking God to change our character to be more like God's.

- o When have you called on God's name for a specific purpose?
- o How did God respond?

o What did this experience teach you about God's character?

o How has your character changed as a result?

8. Often we find that something powerful has happened within us while we were waiting. Waiting for the blessing often is part of the blessing itself, since we have to rely on God in new and unexpected ways. Have three volunteers read aloud these stories of others in the Bible who waited: Genesis 8:6-14; 1 Samuel 1:1-20; Luke 2:25-35.

o What do you learn from each of their stories?

o How do you see blessing in the waiting in these stories?

9. Their first encounter with God in Genesis 12 leaves Abram and Sarai in awe of the greatest power in the universe. Their response to hearing the life-changing promises that are to come is to build an altar and call on the name of the Lord. Read aloud Genesis 12:7-8. Building an altar implies both worship and sacrifice. Calling on God's name meant that God's plan and priorities were essential to the future they were seeking.

o Look up these other instances in Scripture of people calling on the name of the Lord: Psalm 86:3-5 and Romans 10:13. What do you learn from each passage?

o When Jesus taught the disciples to pray in Matthew 6: 5-14, how did he teach them to open each prayer? How were they to call on God's name (verse 9)?

10. What God wants to say to us is this: I have a story to tell through you, and my story is better than the story that you've been living.

o Read aloud Hebrews 12:1-2. How is Jesus the author and "perfecter" of our faith?

o What do these verses say about God's role in our stories?

Deeper Conversation (10-15 minutes)

In advance, write the following on a board or chart paper. Divide into groups of two or three for deeper conversation.

- How has God brought blessings into your life in the following three categories?
  1. People who've brought joy to your life.
  2. Places you've treasured.
  3. The presence of God with you in good times and bad.

Closing Prayer (3 minutes)

Close the session by taking personal prayer requests from group members and leading the group in prayer. When you close later sessions, encourage those in the group to participate in the Closing Prayer by praying aloud for one another and the requests given.

Session 2

JACOB AND ESAU

Bible Story Overview

After years of infertility and a trying pregnancy (Scripture tells us that the babies "struggled" within her), Rebekah gave birth to twins. She and her husband, Isaac, named their firstborn Esau, which means "Hairy," because he was covered from head to toe with red hair. As Esau was born they noticed that a little hand was tightly gripping his heel, so they named their second born Jacob, which means "Grabby." Actually, *Jacob* means not only "Grabby" but also "Deceiver," "Taker of What Is Not His," and these unfortunate connotations would have a deep impact on the person he would become.

The sibling rivalry between Esau and Jacob, which began in the womb, was fueled by their parents. Rebekah favored Jacob, and Isaac favored Esau. This fostered competition and unhappiness between the brothers. Riddled with envy and discontent—and encouraged by his mother—Jacob deceived his father by pretending to be Esau, so he could receive both the birthright and blessing due the firstborn son. In that moment he lost not only a brother but also any sense of goodness in himself. Jacob spent the first half of his life struggling to take what was not rightfully his and the second half running away from the mistakes he'd made.

Though Jacob found material success in the form of wives, children, livestock, and wealth, none of it seemed to satisfy him. So, years after running away, he decided to face the consequences of his actions and return home. On the last leg of his journey, before he came upon Esau, he sent his entourage on ahead and sat down alone. That night he had a divine encounter that forced him to grab hold of God! A mysterious man appeared in the middle of the night and wrestled with Jacob until sunrise. Jacob was bold enough to ask his wrestling partner for a blessing. His opponent told him that his name would no longer be Jacob but Israel—"He Who Wrestles with God." Jacob became Israel. The nation once promised to Abraham and Sarah now had a name— the children of Israel, the ones who wrestle with God.

Main Point

Regardless of our pasts, God has the power to rewrite our stories, showering us with grace and blessing us, even when we don't deserve it. We can trust that God will continue perfecting the story that God is writing in us.

Key Scriptures

> *These are the descendants of Isaac, Abraham's son:*
> *Abraham was the father of Isaac, and Isaac was forty*
> *years old when he married Rebekah, daughter of Bethuel*
> *the Aramean of Paddan-aram, sister of Laban the*
> *Aramean. Isaac prayed to the* LORD *for his wife, because she*
> *was barren; and the* LORD *granted his prayer, and his wife*
> *Rebekah conceived. The children struggled together within*

her; and she said, "If it is to be this way, why do I live?" So she went to inquire of the LORD. And the LORD said to her,

> *"Two nations are in your womb,*
> *and two peoples born of you shall be divided;*
> *the one shall be stronger than the other,*
> *the elder shall serve the younger."*

When her time to give birth was at hand, there were twins in her womb. The first came out red, all his body like a hairy mantle; so they named him Esau. Afterward his brother came out, with his hand gripping Esau's heel; so he was named Jacob. Isaac was sixty years old when she bore them.
> *(Genesis 25:19-26)*

What You Will Need

- *The Rewritten Life* DVD and DVD player
- Markerboard or chart paper and markers

SESSION OUTLINE

Opening Prayer (3 minutes)

Lead the following prayer or one of your own:

Dear God,

We give you thanks that you are a God of grace, mercy, and redemption. We praise you that you are a God of second chances, do-overs, and fresh starts. We have been hurt by the words and actions of others and by our own choices and mistakes. Yet you have the power to bring healing and to start us on a better path. Help us to remember that regardless of our pasts, you promise to shower us with grace, meet our needs, and bring blessing from every circumstance, even when we don't deserve it—all because we are your children. Teach us humility, contentment, and surrender. We desire to trust you with all of our hearts. In Jesus' name we pray. Amen.

Discussion Starter (5 minutes)

Use the following question as an icebreaker, inviting group members to give short "popcorn" answers:

- What is a nickname you have been called over the years? How does this nickname reflect, or not reflect, the story of your life?

Video (7 minutes)

Play the Session 2 video segment on the DVD.

Video Discussion and Bible Study (30 minutes)

More discussion points, questions, and Bible study questions have been provided than you will have time to include. Before the session, select those you want to cover, and put a check mark beside them.

1. Most biblical names were given with one of two purposes: to mark the circumstances surrounding a person's birth, or to describe specific character traits or gifts the child would grow to have.
   o How did Rebekah and Isaac adhere to these guidelines when naming their twin sons, Esau and Jacob?
   o How did Jacob's life and character reflect the meaning of his name?

2. Close family members, such as siblings, often are our first indication that the world doesn't revolve around us. Our relationships with these family members can define who we are and how we will treat others throughout our lives.
   o How would you describe the relationship between Esau and Jacob? What contributed to the discord and conflict between them?

o How did Jacob take advantage of Esau? What, do you think, were his motivations?

o What were some of the long-term effects of his deception?

o Have someone read aloud Philippians 2:3-4 and Romans 12:10. When have you, like Jacob, struggled to consider others better than yourself and to put their needs first?

3. One day when Jacob saw the moment to take advantage of his brother, he grabbed it. Have someone read aloud Genesis 25:27-34. Discuss the following questions:

o What did Esau ask of Jacob?

o What did Jacob ask for in return, and how did he guarantee it?

o How did Jacob take advantage of Esau in this situation?

o How did Esau respond?

4. As twins, Jacob and Esau had a very close connection. They also were tempted by competition and contempt. The closer we are to the people in our lives, the more our familiarity can tempt us or give us an excuse to treat them with disrespect. At the same time, our closeness allows us to discover the amazing gifts God places in each individual. The relationships that are part of your everyday life have the potential to make you jealous like Jacob, or you can choose to celebrate the gift of your close relationships and the handiwork of God you find there.

o Do you tend to be more of a "Jealous Jacob" or a person who chooses to celebrate the gifts and abilities you see in others? Why?

o Think of three important people in your life. What are some hidden gifts that each person brings to your life? What can you do to affirm these gifts?

o   Take turns reading aloud the followings passages,
summarizing the message of each as it relates to how we
are to treat each other:
- ► Luke 6:31
- ► Romans 15:7
- ► 1 Corinthians 1:10
- ► Galatians 6:2
- ► Ephesians 4:2-3
- ► 1 Thessalonians 5:11

5. Jacob made the mistake of determining his happiness based
on what his brother had. Our worth isn't determined by how
we measure up against other people; it is determined by how
God loves us.

o   What is an area of your life in which you struggle to be
content?

o   How can focusing on what others have keep us from
being content with our blessings?

o   Read aloud 1 John 4:7-12, 19-21. What is the relationship
between God's love for us and our love for others?

o   How would you define or explain *favoritism*?

6. God never operates according to the principle of scarcity.
God is never limited in how many prayers God can answer
or how much love God can pour out. Just because God loves
and blesses one of God's children doesn't mean God can't
love and bless all the others. In fact, God knows specifically
how to offer each of us answers to our unique needs. Have
someone read aloud Psalm 50:7-12; Matthew 7:7-12; and
Ephesians 3:19; then discuss the following:

o   What do these verses say about the abundance and
generosity of our heavenly Parent?

o   In what ways is God the best model of a parent that we can look to?

7. On the very last leg of his journey, Jacob learned that he was about to encounter the one person he needed to make amends with: his brother, Esau. The night before the confrontation, Jacob took everything he had accumulated—everything and everyone he had grabbed, deceived, or swindled to get—and sent them across a river called Jabbok, which means "emptying." Then he sat down alone.

    o   Read aloud Genesis 32:24. Who wrestled with Jacob?
    o   Read aloud Genesis 32:27. When Jacob asked for a blessing, what did his wrestling partner ask him, and what was Jacob's answer?
    o   Read aloud Genesis 32:28. What new name did God give Jacob, and why?
    o   Read aloud Genesis 32:29-30. What did Jacob ask his wrestling partner? What answer did Jacob's wrestling partner give (verse 29)? What did Jacob name the place, and why (verse 30)?

8. God wants to hear our honest confession and assessment of who we are and where we find ourselves, but that doesn't mean God will leave us that way. Only when we are honest about our desperate state and need can God set about changing us to become the ones God wants us to be.

    o   How can "wrestling with God" help us find the peace, forgiveness, and transformation we long for?
    o   Has there been a time when you knew without a doubt that God was with you? If so, describe how you knew at the time, or how you know now in retrospect, that God joined you in your struggle.

Deeper Conversation (10-15 minutes)

In advance, write the following on a board or chart paper. Divide participants into smaller groups of two or three for deeper conversation.

- According to a popular saying, gratitude is the "antidote" to discontent. Talk about some of the things in your life that you are most grateful for. Why are you so grateful for these things?

Closing Prayer (3 minutes)

Close the session by taking personal prayer requests from group members and leading the group in prayer. Encourage those in the group to participate in the Closing Prayer by praying aloud for one another and the requests given.

Session 3

NAOMI

Bible Story Overview

We find Naomi's story in a book of the Bible named for someone else, her daughter-in-law Ruth. As we learn in four short chapters, their stories are intertwined as Ruth chose to remain with Naomi after the devastating loss of Naomi's husband and two sons, one of whom was Ruth's husband. This tragedy, coming on the heels of a famine that had caused Naomi and her family to abandon their homeland and move to a foreign land, was too much to bear. Discouraged and despairing, Naomi decided that her name, which means "Pleasant," no longer fit. So she renamed herself Mara, which means "Bitter," blaming God for the devastation she had experienced.

After returning to Naomi's hometown of Bethlehem (sound familiar?), Ruth went to the fields to glean, working tirelessly until the end of the harvest. Her initiative and hard work saved both her life and

Naomi's, setting into motion a course of events that would change their lives and the story of God's people forever.

Ruth's heart of service toward Naomi inspired Boaz, the owner of the field where Ruth gleaned, to help her. Boaz happened to be Naomi's kinsman-redeemer—a role given by the law in Leviticus to a man who would help a family member in distress by "redeeming" them. As Naomi watched Ruth's tireless hard work and kindness and learned of Boaz's acts of compassion, she awoke from her fog of grief, never to be known by Mara again.

Naomi devised a plan to get Boaz to fulfill his role as kinsman-redeemer, which meant purchasing the land that belonged to their family and marrying Ruth. Her plan worked, and their family was restored to financial health and good standing in the community. Boaz and Ruth's first child, Obed, became the great-grandfather of David, the most influential king Israel ever knew, and a forefather of Jesus himself, the long-awaited Messiah. What appeared to be a happy ending for Naomi was actually the beginning of a new and much grander story than she ever could have imagined.

Main Point

God wants to be part of both the good and bad parts of our lives and invites us to share our deepest struggles. God promises to walk with us during difficult times. Even when our stories seem hopeless, God is at work behind the scenes.

Key Scriptures

> *In the days when the judges ruled, there was a famine in the land, and a certain man of Bethlehem in Judah went to live in the country of Moab, he and his wife and two sons. The name of the man was Elimelech and the name of his wife Naomi, and the names of his two sons were Mahlon and Chilion; they were Ephrathites from Bethlehem in Judah. They went into the country of Moab and remained*

there. But Elimelech, the husband of Naomi, died, and she was left with her two sons. These took Moabite wives; the name of the one was Orpah and the name of the other Ruth. When they had lived there about ten years, both Mahlon and Chilion also died, so that the woman was left without her two sons and her husband.

Then she started to return with her daughters-in-law from the country of Moab, for she had heard in the country of Moab that the LORD had considered his people and given them food. So she set out from the place where she had been living, she and her two daughters-in-law, and they went on their way to go back to the land of Judah. But Naomi said to her two daughters-in-law, "Go back each of you to your mother's house. May the LORD deal kindly with you, as you have dealt with the dead and with me. The LORD grant that you may find security, each of you in the house of your husband." Then she kissed them, and they wept aloud. They said to her, "No, we will return with you to your people." But Naomi said, "Turn back, my daughters, why will you go with me? Do I still have sons in my womb that they may become your husbands? Turn back, my daughters, go your way, for I am too old to have a husband. Even if I thought there was hope for me, even if I should have a husband tonight and bear sons, would you then wait until they were grown? Would you then refrain from marrying? No, my daughters, it has been far more bitter for me than for you, because the hand of the LORD has turned against me." Then they wept aloud again. Orpah kissed her mother-in-law, but Ruth clung to her.

(Ruth 1:1-14)

What You Will Need

- *The Rewritten Life* DVD and DVD player
- Markerboard or chart paper and markers

SESSION OUTLINE

Opening Prayer (3 minutes)

Lead the following prayer or one of your own:

Dear God,

Thank you for inviting us to share our deepest struggles with you. We're so grateful that you are with us in both the good times and the bad times and that you promise to see us through even the darkest moments. Thank you for always being at work in our lives. Give us eyes that see your work, no matter how hidden it may seem, and hearts that trust you to be there. And teach us to look beyond our own circumstances and needs to those of others. We ask these things in Jesus' name. Amen.

Discussion Starter (5 minutes)

Use the following question as an icebreaker, inviting group members to give short "popcorn" answers:

- What does your name mean? Would you say this meaning is an accurate description of your personality? Why, or why not?

Video (7 minutes)

Play the Session 3 video segment on the DVD.

Video Discussion and Bible Study (30 minutes)

More discussion points, questions, and Bible study questions have been provided than you will have time to include. Before the session, select those you want to cover, and put a check mark beside them.

1. Naomi's life was torn apart when she lost everything she
    had known and loved. Ask someone to read aloud
    Ruth 1:1-4, 19-21.
    o   Why did Naomi change her name after returning to
        Bethlehem? What did her new name, *Mara*, mean?
    o   How do we know that Naomi blamed God for her tragic
        circumstances? Why do you think she did this?
    o   Is there a time when Naomi's new name, *Bitter*, applied
        to your life? Have you ever turned your anger, blame, or
        bitterness toward God? How did you handle it? How did
        those feelings change over time?

2. Read Ruth 1:13. Then, have some volunteers read Psalms
    22:1-2, 44:23-24, and 88:1-18 in which people struggled
    honestly with their feelings toward God.
    o   How does Naomi think that God feels toward her?
    o   Are her emotions surprising to you? Why, or why not?
    o   Why, do you think, are they included in Holy Scripture?

3. God desires an authentic relationship with us. God wants to
    know our hearts and have us express ourselves honestly.
    o   How do the psalms we just read (see above, #2)
        encourage us to pour out our hearts freely to God?
    o   What does Naomi's story teach us about expressing our
        pain and frustration and about being honest with God?

4. Have someone read aloud Ruth 1:16-18. With these words,
    Ruth formed a covenant friendship with Naomi. Ruth and
    Naomi's bond was severed by the death of Ruth's husband,
    Naomi's son. Ruth's covenant reinstated their family
    connection. Stronger than a contract, Ruth's covenant had
    at its center the God that she and her mother-in-law would
    both worship and follow. They would need God's strength to
    carry them through the difficult days ahead.

31

- o What is a *covenant friendship*? How does Ruth's relationship with Naomi exemplify this kind of friendship?
- o How do Ruth's words bind her not only to Naomi but also to Naomi's God?
- o How might having common faith have helped Ruth and Naomi support one another?
- o Why is it important for us to nurture friendships with others who share our faith in Jesus Christ?

5. Ruth made an alliance of friendship with Naomi that went beyond bloodlines and marriage. She chose to reject ties with family members in order to support and protect a friend. Covenant friendship often runs deeper than ties with relatives.
- o Have you ever had to reject the beliefs or habits of your family? If so, were there friends whose lives and decisions you identified with more closely than your family ties?
- o Are there people in your life whom you have made your family of choice (those who are not related to you but whom you treat like family)? If so, how have those friendships sustained you in life?

6. Ruth must have experienced the same kind of pain and tears that Naomi did. She may have even gone through similar stages of anger and depression. But we see in Chapter 2 that Ruth's grief took on a different shape. Instead of wallowing or waiting for someone else to take responsibility, Ruth channeled her grief, worry, and anxiety into action.
- o Read Ruth 2:2. What does Ruth request as soon as she and Naomi return to Bethlehem?
- o Read Ruth 2:7. What do we learn about Ruth's work ethic?

o When you've been faced with circumstances that overwhelmed you, how did you respond? Do you identify more with Naomi's reaction of being rendered inactive, frozen by her circumstances, or Ruth's "get-up-and-go" tendency to take care of it herself?

7. Boaz, the owner of the fields in which Ruth worked each day, noticed her determination. He perceived that Ruth was a remarkable young woman. He saw that she wasn't wallowing in self-pity or waiting for someone to take care of her problems for her. And her take-charge attitude inspired Boaz to help her succeed.

   o Read Ruth 2:5-16. Name the things that Boaz does for Ruth out of kindness.

   o Why does he tell her he is doing these things (verses 11-12)?

8. Ruth acted with selflessness, serving Naomi. Boaz acted with integrity, serving and protecting Ruth. Naomi came up with a plan that had daring audacity—one that would serve to reward Ruth for her kindness and ensure a future with hope for all of them.

   o When have you have seen people help others by acting with audacity (as Naomi does), with integrity (as Boaz does), or with submission and selflessness (as Ruth does)?

9. God loves to work in anonymous ways and then watch us uncover God's goodness. God is working not only for our good—for each of our small stories—but also for the good of God's creation—for the big story that is always greater than anything we can wrap our minds around.

   o How is the happy ending of Naomi's story a beginning of a new and grander story?

o   Have some volunteers read aloud John 20:13-17, Luke 24:30-32, Matthew 25:31-40, Hebrews 13:2, and Romans 8:28. How is God at work in these Scriptures? How do these verses relate to Ruth and Naomi's story?

10. Fairy tales encourage us to place our hope in fantasies of rescue and romance. Scripture encourages us to place our hope in the Lord. Even though there is a kinsman-redeemer in Naomi and Ruth's story, he is an instrument of God and a representation of the true Kinsman-Redeemer—Jesus Christ.

o   How would you define or explain the role of a *goel* or kinsman-redeemer?

o   In what ways is God our *Goel*—our Kinsman-Redeemer? Review and discuss the following Scripture passages: Genesis 1:27; Exodus 6:6; Psalm 49:15; Isaiah 43:1; Ephesians 2:13; 1 Peter 1:18-19; 1 John 3:1-2.

o   How have you seen God come to the rescue as a Redeemer?

Deeper Conversation (10-15 minutes)

Beforehand, write the following on a board or chart paper. Divide into smaller groups of two or three for deeper conversation.

•   What surprised you about Naomi's story? What new things did you learn as you read the Book of Ruth?

Closing Prayer (3 minutes)

Close the session by taking personal prayer requests from group members and leading the group in prayer. Encourage those in the group to participate in the Closing Prayer by praying aloud for one another and the requests given.

Session 4

DANIEL

Bible Story Overview

Under the leadership of King Nebuchadnezzar, the Babylonians invaded Jerusalem in 605 B.C., destroying the city and the Temple, the place where the Israelites worshiped—and where they believed God resided in a unique and special way. Four young Hebrews who may have been in their teens—Daniel, Hananiah, Mishael, and Azariah—were among those captured and taken to Babylon. Hananiah, Mishael, and Azariah are better known by their Babylonian names: Shadrach, Meshach, and Abednego.

Nebuchadnezzar's strategy was to destroy the culture and convert the people by taking an entire generation of leaders back to Babylon, where they would be treated not as prisoners-of-war or slaves but as trainees for positions of leadership, influence, and power. The captives were offered a new and lavish lifestyle, complete with delicacies of food and drink. While this offer of exotic tastes may have enticed some of the exiles, Daniel and his friends weren't interested. The food they were being offered had been sacrificed and dedicated to idols. By eating it they would have betrayed God. These young men stood up to the Babylonians, deprived themselves of one lavish meal after another, and remained true to their God.

Later when Shadrach, Meshach, and Abednego also refused to bow down and worship the ninety-foot-high golden statue King Nebuchadnezzar had built, they were thrown into a blazing furnace heated to seven times hotter than usual. The guards who put the three young men into the furnace were engulfed in flames, but Shadrach, Meshach, and Abednego entered the furnace without being singed. Those who looked into the furnace saw not only the three Hebrews but also a fourth man. None had been burned. Nebuchadnezzar knew that Shadrach, Meshach, and Abednego's God had protected them. When he called them out of the furnace, he praised their God and promoted them in his service.

On another occasion a decree was passed that no one was to pray to any god or anyone other than King Darius, a later king of Babylon. When Daniel was seen praying three times a day through a window of his room that pointed toward Jerusalem, he was arrested and thrown into a lions' den. The next morning when King Darius rushed to find out what had happened, he found Daniel unharmed. He then issued a decree that everyone in his kingdom must "fear and reverence the God of Daniel" (Daniel 6:26 NIV).

Again and again the leaders of Babylon tried to force Daniel and his friends to take God from the center of their lives and put false gods and idols in God's place. They even changed the young men's names—replacing their God-honoring names with names that had Babylonian gods at the center. (You know Shadrach, Meshach, and Abednego. Daniel was given the name Belteshazzar.) Yet Daniel and his friends remained true to their faith and their God, continuing to worship him even when it meant risking their lives.

Main Point

Our culture continually invites us to give our hearts and lives to something other than God, but we are not alone when it comes to following God in this world. We have the Holy Spirit within us to guide us, the teachings of those who have led us to God to sustain us, and the examples of the faithful to inspire and encourage us.

Key Scriptures

In the third year of the reign of King Jehoiakim of Judah, King Nebuchadnezzar of Babylon came to Jerusalem and besieged it. The Lord let King Jehoiakim of Judah fall into his power, as well as some of the vessels of the house of God. These he brought to the land of Shinar, and placed the vessels in the treasury of his gods.

Then the king commanded his palace master Ashpenaz to bring some of the Israelites of the royal family and of the nobility, young men without physical defect and handsome, versed in every branch of wisdom, endowed with knowledge and insight, and competent to serve in the king's palace; they were to be taught the literature and language of the Chaldeans. The king assigned them a daily portion of the royal rations of food and wine. They were to be educated for three years, so that at the end of that time they could be stationed in the king's court. Among them were Daniel, Hananiah, Mishael, and Azariah, from the tribe of Judah. The palace master gave them other names: Daniel he called Belteshazzar, Hananiah he called Shadrach, Mishael he called Meshach, and Azariah he called Abednego.

But Daniel resolved that he would not defile himself with the royal rations of food and wine; so he asked the palace master to allow him not to defile himself. Now God allowed Daniel to receive favor and compassion from the palace master. The palace master said to Daniel, "I am afraid of my lord the king; he has appointed your food and your drink. If he should see you in poorer condition than the other young men of your own age, you would endanger my head with the king." Then Daniel asked the guard whom the palace master had appointed over Daniel, Hananiah, Mishael, and Azariah: "Please test your servants for ten days. Let us be given vegetables to eat and water to drink. You can then compare our appearance with the appearance of the young men who eat the royal rations, and deal with your servants according to what you observe." So he agreed to this proposal and tested them for ten days. At the end of ten days it was observed that they appeared better and fatter than all the young men who had been eating the royal rations. So the guard continued to withdraw their royal rations and the wine they were to drink, and gave them vegetables. To these four young men God gave knowledge and skill in every aspect of literature and wisdom; Daniel also had insight into all visions and dreams.

At the end of the time that the king had set for them to be brought in, the palace master brought them into the presence of Nebuchadnezzar, and the king spoke with them. And among them all, no one was found to compare with Daniel, Hananiah, Mishael, and Azariah; therefore they were stationed in the king's court. In every matter of wisdom and understanding concerning which the king inquired of them, he found them ten times better than all the magicians and enchanters in his whole kingdom. And Daniel continued there until the first year of King Cyrus.

(Daniel 1:1-21)

What You Will Need

- *The Rewritten Life* DVD and DVD player
- Markerboard or chart paper and markers

SESSION OUTLINE

Opening Prayer (3 minutes)

Lead the following prayer or one of your own:

Dear God,

It's not easy living in a culture that continually pressures us to conform to practices, customs, beliefs, and attitudes that do not honor you. It's hard standing for you when the rest of the world seems to be bowing down to anything and everything other than you. Give us the courage and strength to be faithful. Help us to recognize any idols in our lives—things we put in the seat that you alone should occupy. Forgive us for making relationships or control, worry or financial resources, jobs or children, food or sex, status or wealth the center of our thoughts and priorities. Lord, so transform us that our lives draw attention to you. We want to bring honor and praise to the name of Jesus. Amen.

Discussion Starter (5 minutes)

Use the following question as an icebreaker, inviting group members to give short "popcorn" answers:

- What story from your life qualifies as epic? Maybe a family road trip or a holiday? Maybe a near-death experience?

Video (7 minutes)

Play the Session 4 video segment on the DVD.

Video Discussion and Bible Study (30 minutes)

Note that more discussion points, questions, and Bible study questions have been provided than you will have time to include. Before the session, select those you want to cover, and put a check mark beside them.

1. Newborns receive messages about how structured or chaotic, loud or quiet, loving or distant the family's culture will be. Families teach some of the same lessons, but each of our families is unique in some ways, with its own values, standards, and habits that make it special. Your own family, for example, may have communicated the importance of getting an education, appreciating music or nature, serving the poor, or respecting the wisdom of elders.
   o What kinds of messages and methods do you think are most effective for teaching children to follow God regardless of the messages they receive from the world? What kinds are least effective?
   o What are some of the unique lessons, values, or habits that you learned growing up?
   o What did you learn from the adults in your life about what kind of story your family would tell?

2. When Babylon invaded and destroyed Jerusalem in 605 B.C., King Nebuchadnezzar's plan was to destroy the culture and convert the people by taking an entire generation of leaders back to Babylon, where they would be trained for positions of leadership, influence, and power.
   o Read Daniel 1:3-5 and 1:8-17. How were Daniel, Hananiah, Mishael, and Azariah pressured to conform to the Babylonian culture, and how did they respond? Why, do you think, did they respond this way?
   o In what ways does our culture invite us to give our hearts and lives to something besides God?

3. The Babylonians took the names that these young men's parents had given them to honor God and replaced them with names that honored the idols worshiped in Babylon. Some of the changes even deliberately mocked their original names and the God they had been raised to worship. They became, *Belteshazzar*, *Shadrach*, *Meshach*, and *Abednego*. Just to give you an idea of how awful the name change was, Mishael, which means "Who Is Like Yahweh?" became Meshach, "Who Is Like Aku?" And not only were they renamed; their first meal called their beliefs into question.
   o Daniel and his friends faced a tough opposition to their faithfulness to God. When have you faced opposition to your faith? What happened?
   o What are some of the emotions the young men must have struggled through as their names were changed and they were forced to renounce their faith in God?
   o Read the following Scriptures: Numbers 32:20-24; Matthew 6:6, 18; Luke 8:16-17. What does each say about what we do in secret, even if no one knows but God and us?

4. Hananiah, Mishael, and Azariah (better known as Shadrach, Meshach, and Abednego) soon faced an even bigger challenge—whether to bow down to the ninety-foot-high golden idol statue built by King Nebuchadnezzar. While their decision about meals was known only to a few, their refusal to bow was a bold, public act—one that resulted in their being thrown into a fiery furnace. Just because they did the right thing in God's eyes did not mean they were immune to the earthly consequences of their actions, however unfair.
   o What happened to Hananiah, Mishael, and Azariah? How was God with them in the midst of this trial?

o   Although we can't always be sure of our earthly safety
    because we are God's followers, what can we always
    be sure of? How have you experienced God's presence
    during a difficult time?

o   How hard is it for you to make God-honoring choices
    when those choices will make you look or seem
    "peculiar" to everyone else? Describe a time when you
    had to make a hard decision about doing what is right
    and honoring God, whether privately or publicly.

5. In an attempt to trap Daniel, his enemies orchestrated a
    decree from the king that said no one could worship or pray
    to anyone but the king for a month. Daniel's friends had
    faced a law that had forced them to worship something false;
    now he faced a law forcing him *not* to worship something
    true. Yet Daniel remained faithful in his daily habit of prayer,
    even when it meant his life was at stake. His continual
    seeking of God's heart through worship helped him do what
    was right even when his life was at stake.

o   What was the consequence of Daniel disobeying the
    king's decree? What happened?

o   How would you say that Daniel's private worship
    prepared him to face the lions' den?

o   Read aloud Exodus 25:8-9, Psalm 100, and Revelation
    4:1-11. What do these Scriptures, from different parts of
    the Bible, say about the importance of worship?

o   How does worshiping with brothers and sisters of faith
    encourage and equip us to remain faithful in times of
    temptation and trial?

6. The leaders of Babylon tried to force Daniel, Hananiah,
    Mishael, and Azariah to take God from the center of their
    lives and put false gods and idols in God's place. Since the
    true God held a place of honor in their names, they were

given new names with false gods, idols, in that place of honor and esteem.

o   Read aloud Psalm 115:4-8, Matthew 4:8–10, and Romans 1:21-23. What do these verses teach us about making idols and worshiping false gods?

o   What problems do we have with idol worship today? What are the idols we commonly worship in our culture—things that draw our attention, money, and passion in a way that diminishes our love for God?

o   What are things in your own life that attract you to pay greater attention to them than you do to God?

7.   When we enter into relationship with God, we are given the incredible privilege of wearing God's name. We become the face of God to the people we meet, God's representatives on earth.

o   Have someone read aloud 1 Corinthians 3:16-17, 2 Corinthians 5:18-21, and Colossians 3:15-17. What do these verses teach us about being God's representatives?

o   How do you feel about being God's representative to the world? How might others see "the face of God" in your life?

o   Both King Nebuchadnezzar and King Darius had a huge change of heart by the end of their stories in the Book of Daniel. What factors do you think brought about this change in each of them?

8.   Who God is and what God does are in perfect harmony. God's character determines what God does, and what God does demonstrates God's character to the world. We never have to second-guess God because we know he will always act justly and rightly. There is integrity and consistency between who God is and what God does. We can count on God.

o   Read aloud the following statement (you also might write it on a markerboard or chart paper): *Our character determines our actions, and our actions demonstrate our character.* Then read aloud Luke 6:43-45. How have you found this to be true in your own experience and your observation of others?

o   What comes to mind when you hear the word *sanctification*, the process of being made holy? In what ways does God sanctify us?

o   How do we, by living as holy and sanctified followers of Christ, bear witness to the character of God?

o   How have the things that God has done in your life had an impact on the lives of others? How has God been glorified through what God has done in your life?

9. The famous account of Shadrach, Meshach, and Abednego ends with the three of them walking out of the fiery furnace unsinged and unharmed. King Nebuchadnezzar, who had ordered them burned to death, was impressed, but he wasn't impressed with Shadrach, Meshach, and Abednego. Rather, he saw in them the work of the God whom they served.

o   Read Daniel 3:28-29. What is the king's reaction to what transpired in the fiery furnace?

o   Remember that this is the same king who'd had a golden statue of himself built and demanded that everyone in Babylon bow down to it. What, do you think, changed his attitude?

10. A similar change occurred in another Babylonian king some years later. King Darius decreed that no one could pray to any god, person, or thing but him. When Daniel disobeyed this decree, Darius had him thrown into a den of lions.

o   Read Daniel 6:17-23.What do they do to ensure that Daniel cannot escape the lions' den?

o What does King Darius find when he rushes to the lions' den the next morning?

o Whom, does Daniel say, shut the mouths of the lions?

11. When Daniel survived a night in the lions' den, King Darius changed his tune completely. Instead of demanding that all people pray only to the king, he issued another decree.

o Read Daniel 6:25-27. What does the king discover about God?

o What does he decree that people must do?

o Remember that this is the same king who issued a decree demanding that people pray only to him. What, do you think, caused his change of heart?

12. God calls us to live so differently from the people around us so that they will take notice. Specifically God calls us to emulate Jesus. Daniel, Hananiah, Mishael, and Azariah had God's name embedded in their own names. When we make a pledge to follow Jesus, God gives us the name "Christian" to wear—a title that has the very name of Christ embedded in it. If we allow God to continually transform our hearts and actions, the story of our lives will bring honor and praise not to ourselves but to Christ.

o When have your actions hurt God's reputation instead of helping it?

o When have your actions called attention to the power, love, and character of God instead of to yourself?

o Read Matthew 5:13-16. Whom will people praise when they see our good deeds?

o How do the stories of Daniel and his friends encourage you to trust God with your story?

Deeper Conversation (10-15 minutes)

In advance, write the following on a markerboard or large sheet of paper. Divide into smaller groups of two or three for deeper conversation.

- Take a good look at your daily and weekly routines. What things have become idols in your life? What things consume your time, thoughts, and energy? How can God be a more present part of your everyday life?

Closing Prayer (3 minutes)

Close the session by taking personal prayer requests from group members and leading the group in prayer. Encourage those in the group to participate in the Closing Prayer by praying aloud for one another and the requests given.

Session 5

PETER

Bible Story Overview

When Simon answered the call to follow Jesus, he was a mess. He was impulsive, brash, immature, and reckless. His temper flared and he usually spoke before he could think about what was coming from his mouth. Simon might have seemed an unlikely choice to be one of Jesus' twelve disciples, but Jesus saw the potential in him. Not only was Simon chosen to be one of a dozen of Jesus' closest followers, but he also was selected to be a leader among the disciples and a leader of the ragtag collection of imperfect people who would come to be called the church. Because of his impulsive nature, Simon was often willing to take risks the others did not want to take.

At times his risky, erratic behavior got him into trouble. But because Simon often was willing to take risks that others would not, there were times when his impulsivity was right on the mark. When

47

Jesus asked the disciples, "Who do *you* say that I am?" all hesitated except Simon. He responded immediately, "You are the Christ, the Son of the living God" (Matthew 16:16 NASB). Jesus acknowledged that God had revealed this to Simon; then Jesus changed Simon's name to Peter, which means "Rock" or "Boulder." Jesus told him, "On this rock I will build my church" (Matthew 16:18).

Not long after this high point in his relationship with Jesus, Simon—now Peter—experienced one of his lowest lows. On Jesus' final evening with Peter and the other disciples, Jesus offered to wash each of his disciples' feet. Instead of embracing the moment or waiting to see what Jesus might be trying to teach him, Peter recoiled and rebuked Jesus, saying, "You will never wash my feet" (John 13:8). But when Jesus explained the purpose of the foot-washing, Peter had a change of heart and begged for Jesus to wash not only his feet, but all of him. Again Peter's impulsivity brought to light both the worst and the best in his heart.

During this time Jesus also told Peter that Satan had "asserted the right to sift" the disciples "like wheat" (Luke 22:31 CEB) but that he had prayed that his followers' faith would not fail. Peter puffed himself up with characteristic bravado and declared that he was ready to face prison or even death for Jesus' sake. Yet, just as Jesus predicted, Peter wound up denying him later that night not once, but three times. This all happened just hours before Jesus died a humiliating death on the cross. One day after Peter hit his lowest point, Jesus—whom Peter had denied and failed—appeared to be gone. But there was more to Jesus' story, and to Peter's. Following his resurrection, Jesus met Peter and the other disciples on the seashore one morning and gave Peter the opportunity to affirm his love for him not once, but three times.

Like Peter, many of us have stories that are full of highs and lows, ups and downs, failures and triumphs. His story reminds us that we don't have to be perfect in order for God to use us, and that, while we may be impulsive and erratic, God's love for us never is.

Main Point

Even as we walk with God, we sometimes will fall. But there is always grace, forgiveness, and hope. God patiently transforms us, making us more and more like Jesus, in a slow movement of grace that takes a lifetime.

Key Scriptures

> *Now when Jesus came into the district of Caesarea Philippi, he asked his disciples, "Who do people say that the Son of Man is?" And they said, "Some say John the Baptist, but others Elijah, and still others Jeremiah or one of the prophets." He said to them, "But who do you say that I am?" Simon Peter answered, "You are the Messiah, the Son of the living God."And Jesus answered him, "Blessed are you, Simon son of Jonah! For flesh and blood has not revealed this to you, but my Father in heaven. And I tell you, you are Peter, and on this rock I will build my church, and the gates of Hades will not prevail against it."*
>
> *(Matthew 16:13-18)*

What You Will Need

- *The Rewritten Life* DVD and a DVD player
- Markerboard or chart paper and markers

SESSION OUTLINE

Opening Prayer (3 minutes)

Lead the following prayer or one of your own:

Dear God,

Thank you for choosing ordinary, imperfect people like Simon Peter to be your followers. We are so grateful for their stories, which remind us we don't have to earn your love and we can never lose your love, because you love us unconditionally and completely just as we are. Even when we make mistakes and choose to disobey, you shower us with grace and mercy, redeeming our failures and turning them into testimonies that show others your gracious and forgiving nature. May we be more like you, Lord, always offering others grace, even when their actions and choices disappoint or hurt us. We ask this in the powerful name of Jesus, who overcame death and who transforms us even now into his own image. In Jesus' name we pray. Amen.

Discussion Starter (5 minutes)

Use the following question as an icebreaker, inviting group members to give short "popcorn" answers:

- What is a nickname that others might give you to describe a characteristic or ability you have? (For example, if you are smart, they might call you "Owl" or "Professor.")

Video (7 minutes)

Play the Session 5 video segment on the DVD.

Video Discussion and Bible Study (30 minutes)

Note that more discussion points, questions, and Bible study questions have been provided than you will have time to include. Before the session, select those you want to cover, and put a check mark beside them.

1. When Simon answered the call to follow Jesus, he was a mess. He was impulsive, brash, immature, and reckless. Jesus knew he had his work cut out for him where Simon was concerned. But Jesus chose Simon nonetheless. Jesus chose him not only to be a disciple but also to be a leader of the movement that would become the church.

    o   Read aloud the lists of Jesus' twelve disciples from Matthew 10:2-4, Mark 3:16-19, Luke 6:13-16, and Acts 1:13-14. Who is always listed first?

    o   Who is listed last in Matthew's, Mark's, and Luke's lists, and what is said about him?

    o   Who is missing from the list in Acts?

2. Despite Simon's impulsiveness and brashness, Jesus saw something in him and chose him to be not only a disciple but also the leader of the disciples.

    o   Have someone read aloud Matthew 16:13-19. Who did Simon say that Jesus was, and who revealed this to Simon? What did Jesus rename Simon, and what did his new name mean?

    o   Have someone read Matthew 16:21-28 aloud. Compare and contrast this outburst with Peter's outburst in Matthew 16:13-18. In what way did Peter go from being a foundation for Jesus' message to a stumbling block? How do we often do the same thing in our own lives?

    o   Why, do you think, did Jesus choose Peter to be the leader of the disciples and of the early church?

3. When it comes to transformation in our lives, most of us would love a microwave solution, one where we could watch change unfolding quickly through a little window. Sometimes that happens. More often, though, God works through the slow movement of grace that takes a lifetime.

    o   Read aloud Mark 14:32-38 and Luke 22:24-34. Why do you think Jesus reverted to using the name *Simon* at these times? In each instance, how was Peter acting like his old self rather than the Rock that Jesus had called him to become?

- o What does Scripture's use of the hybrid name Simon Peter remind us about the process of transformation in our own lives?
- o Sanctification is the process through which we become holy and through which God works within us to make us more like Jesus. Jessica LeGrone in *The Rewritten Life* says that sanctification is "more like a slow cooker than a microwave." In what ways is sanctification more like a slow cooker than a microwave?
- o Where do you see this sort of slow-cooker change in your own life?

4. Living in an imperfect world enables us to see how God deals with disappointment.
   - o How has God responded to your sins and mistakes? What have you learned about God from these responses?
   - o What do these verses teach us about God's grace: Romans 5:1-15; Ephesians 2:8-10; Hebrews 4:16?
   - o Read 1 John 2:12. Why and how have our sins been forgiven?

5. Review the events of the day before Jesus' crucifixion, focusing on Peter: Luke 22:14-20, 24, 33-34; John 13:2-10; Mark 14:32-41; John 18:1-13; and Matthew 26:69-75.
   - o What do these events reveal about Peter?
   - o Read John 21:15-19, in which Jesus appears to his disciples on the seashore. What does Jesus ask Peter, and how does Peter respond? Why, do you think, does Jesus ask the question three times?
   - o Why, do you think, was Jesus more interested in Peter's answer to the question, "Do you love me?" than what Peter had actually done?
   - o How have you experienced God's amazing and restoring grace in response to your mistakes and failures?

6. Learning who God is takes a lifetime of walking with God and searching. Even then we will only fully know God when we finally stand face-to-face.
   o How would you describe the image of God that you had as a child?
   o What have you learned through the years about God's character?
   o How has getting to know the person of Jesus, both through study and your personal relationship with him, helped shape your view of God?

7. Praying in Jesus' name is not a formula that guarantees us the answer we want. It's a sign of intimacy, assuming that we know God well enough to know what kind of prayer would honor his name. It's another way of saying "Thy will be done on earth as it is in heaven," since we're asking for God's will—the things that honor God's name—to become visibly manifest in our world. When we pray in Jesus' name, we should ask ourselves if the prayer reflects our sincere desire to have those things that reflect Jesus' lordship, character, and love done on earth as in heaven.
   o Read Luke 6:46. What does this verse tell us about lordship?
   o Read Matthew 20:27-28 and John 15:13. What do you learn about Jesus' character from these verses?
   o Read John 15:9-12. What do these verses teach us about love?
   o When you pray, how do you determine if your prayer reflects Jesus' love and priorities?

8. Remember that God has a story to tell through you. The story that God is writing is better than the story that you've currently been living.

o   Read aloud Hebrews 12:1-2. In Session 1 we considered what these verses mean. Do you have any new insights about what it means for Jesus to be the "pioneer and perfecter" of our faith?
o   How did Jesus perfect Peter's faith? How did Peter's faith need to be perfected?
o   In what ways does your faith need to be perfected? How is Jesus perfecting your faith?

Deeper Conversation (10-15 minutes)

In advance, write the following on a board or chart. Divide into smaller groups of two or three for deeper conversation.

*   Jesus saw something in Peter that no one, not even Peter, saw in himself. What are some things that others have seen in you that you couldn't see in yourself?

Closing Prayer (3 minutes)

Close the session by taking personal prayer requests from group members and leading the group in prayer. Encourage those in the group to participate in the Closing Prayer by praying aloud for one another and the requests given.

Session 6

An Unnamed Woman

Bible Story Overview

The woman in our story this week is known not by a name but by a label: "The Woman Caught in Adultery." This anonymous woman was dragged before Jesus in the Temple by a group of men who were far too enthusiastic about someone else's sin. It's interesting that the woman's partner isn't also being tried and condemned by this group of legal experts and Pharisees. After all, adultery is a crime that requires two people. Then again these religious leaders seem to have been less concerned with law and justice than with trapping Jesus.

If Jesus had agreed with the Pharisees and experts, he would have upheld the law of Moses but challenged the law of Rome. The Romans, who controlled the Jewish homeland, would have punished him severely. On the other hand, if Jesus had deferred to Roman law, he would have lost the respect of faithful Jewish people who expected the woman to be punished according to their legal traditions. The punishment for adultery was death (Leviticus 20:10), and the religious leaders were prepared to stone the adulterous woman.

The Pharisees and legal experts had Jesus cornered. At the very least, they were sure that they could could split the crowd's opinion of him, sow doubt in the minds of his followers, and reduce the size of his following. If they were successful, they might even set in motion events that would lead not to the woman's execution but to Jesus' death.

Jesus bent down and wrote on the ground with his finger. The text doesn't tell us what he wrote, just that his adversaries continued to badger him with questions. Finally Jesus stood and said, "Let anyone among you who is without sin be the first to throw a stone at her" (John 8:7). Jesus directed the men who had wielded the law like a weapon, against both the woman and against Jesus, to look within their own hearts. They stopped looking at her, or at Jesus, and started looking at themselves. One by one they gave up on trapping Jesus and walked away.

After the woman's accusers left, Jesus asked her, "Where are they? Has no one condemned you?" Then Jesus said, "Neither do I condemn you. Go your way, and from now on do not sin again" (John 8:10-11). Jesus offered the unnamed woman both forgiveness from her past and a new start. He wanted to protect her from the damage her accusers were trying to inflict, but Jesus also was concerned with the damage she was inflicting on herself. He wanted her to be free from sin, but voiced his concern with no hint of condemnation. Throughout the entire ordeal, Jesus demonstrated patience and compassion.

Main Point

God doesn't point out sin because God is against us. God is for us and wants to see us changed for the better. Jesus releases us from condemnation and offers us the freedom to choose a different future.

Key Scriptures

Early in the morning [Jesus] came again to the temple. All the people came to him and he sat down and began to teach them. The scribes and the Pharisees brought a woman who had been caught in adultery; and making her stand before all of them, they said to him, "Teacher, this woman was caught in the very act of committing adultery. Now in the law Moses commanded us to stone such women. Now what do you say?" They said this to test him, so that they might have some charge to bring against him. Jesus bent down and wrote with his finger on the ground. When they kept on questioning him, he straightened up and said to them, "Let anyone among you who is without sin be the first to throw a stone at her." And once again he bent down and wrote on the ground. When they heard it, they went away, one by one, beginning with the elders; and Jesus was left alone with the woman standing before him. Jesus straightened up and said to her, "Woman, where are they? Has no one condemned you?" She said, "No one, sir." And Jesus said, "Neither do I condemn you. Go your way, and from now on do not sin again."

(John 8:2-11)

What You Will Need

- *The Rewritten Life* DVD and a DVD player
- Markerboard or chart paper and markers

SESSION OUTLINE

Opening Prayer (3 minutes)

Lead the following prayer or one of your own:

Dear God,

You have known and loved each one of us since before we were born—before anyone even knew our names. We are humbled and grateful that you know us so intimately and desire a personal relationship with us. Thank you for making that relationship possible through your Son, Jesus, whose love, grace, and forgiveness set us free from the past and call us to a bright new future full of hope and promise. Thank you for loving us as we are, yet loving us too much to leave us that way. We want to become more like Jesus, offering others the same grace we have received. It is in his precious name that we pray. Amen.

Discussion Starter (5 minutes)

Use the following questions as an icebreaker, inviting group members to give short "popcorn" answers:

- When have you felt anonymous or unknown in a group or another situation? How did it make you feel?
- Have you ever felt known or labeled by your latest or worst mistake? How did this make you feel?

Video (7 minutes)

Play the Session 6 video segment on the DVD.

Video Discussion and Bible Study (30 minutes)

Note that more discussion points, questions, and Bible study questions have been provided than you will have time to include. Before the session, select those you want to cover, and put a check mark beside them.

1. The anonymous woman in our story this week is known by a devastating label: "The Woman Caught in Adultery." She was dragged before Jesus in the Temple by a group of men who cared more about trapping Jesus than about sin or justice.
   o How would it feel to be known to posterity by your worst moment(s)?
   o How do we know that the men who accused the unnamed woman were not interested in justice? How were they setting a trap for Jesus?
   o If this woman was not deemed important enough to be remembered by her name, why, do you think, is her story included in the Bible?

2. According to Jewish law, no one could be proven guilty without the testimony of two witnesses. You couldn't just be "the woman accused of adultery" or "the woman suspected of adultery." You had to be caught in the act, and you had to be caught by two eyewitnesses. So it appears these men went to great lengths to have two people catch this woman in the act while, at the same time, letting her partner slip away.
   o Read Deuteronomy 17:6 and 19:15. What were the requirements in the law of Moses for accusing someone of breaking one of the laws or for putting someone to death?
   o Why, do you think, did the religious leaders only bring the woman before Jesus and not her partner?

3. "Jesus bent down and wrote with his finger on the ground" (John 8:6). This made the onlookers curious. What was he writing? The text doesn't tell us. But the Greek verb used for "write" in this verse, *kategraphen*, indicates more than just doodling or drawing. It specifies that Jesus was writing actual words.

- o How did Jesus respond to the religious leaders who brought the unnamed woman before him?
- o What do you think Jesus might have been writing? Why?
- o Read John 8:7-8. After Jesus stood up and spoke to the woman's accusers, what did he do next?

4. The text never questions whether the woman was guilty of the sin of which she was accused. If she was guilty, she was no more guilty than the ones who were using the law against her. Jesus' message that day went much deeper than the dirt in which he wrote. It cut straight to the hearts of those who were watching and listening.
- o Read John 8:7. After Jesus wrote in the dirt the first time, what did he say to the woman's accusers?
- o How would you paraphrase Jesus' words in a way that would be relevant to situations we'd encounter in our culture?

5. In the story of the woman dragged before Jesus for judgment, the men who hauled her there against her will were guilty of a different kind of sin. They were worshiping an idol by worshiping the law itself.
- o How were the woman's accusers guilty of making the law into an idol?
- o Have someone read aloud Ezekiel 6:9-10. Why, do you think, does Ezekiel describe idolatry as spiritual adultery?
- o Have you ever been more concerned about what someone did wrong than you were about that person? Describe what you were thinking and feeling at the time and why you might have been more worried about the transgression than the human being.
- o Have someone read aloud John 8:7. How did Jesus' words redirect the woman's accusers? How did the accusers respond?

6. The accusers in this story were on the attack, using their moral assault on the woman to trap Jesus. We may not pick up rocks to throw at people guilty of sin, but we do hurl critical words, fling disapproving looks, and lob rumors and gossip. Sometimes we disguise these figurative stones as concern or even prayer requests.

   o Have someone read aloud Matthew 7:1-5. When was the last time you found yourself trying to pick a "speck" out of someone else's eye? Are there "specks" that bother you more than others—ones you find yourself frequently judging?

   o Why are we so tempted to focus on others' shortcomings instead of looking within ourselves?

   o How is using the phrase "Love the sinner, hate the sin"— even if filled with good intentions—still an indicator of our outward focus when it comes to sin?

   o How does being honest about our shortcomings and need for God's grace free us?

7. True change is found in discovering who God is, how God and God's love are revealed to us, and how God's grace makes a difference in our own lives. When we call on God's name, we are asking God to change our character to be more like God's.

   o When have you called on God's name for a specific purpose or circumstance?

   o How did you see God at work through that situation?

   o What did you learn about God's unchanging character?

   o In what ways has your character changed as a result?

8. Jesus forgives us and wants to free us from our past and free us for a grace-filled future. Because he doesn't want us to continue on the same path and be damaged by the same

mistakes over and over again, he wants to help us break free from sin's iron grip on our lives.

- o Have someone read aloud John 8:10-11. Rather than giving the woman a verdict, what did Jesus offer her? How did his forgiveness both release her and call her to responsibility?
- o What is the difference between conviction and condemnation? Why is this difference important?
- o Read John 3:17 and Romans 8:1. What do these verses tell us about condemnation?

9. God wants to free us from sin because of God's love for us. Just as a parent hopes to protect children from choices that can hurt them, God will do anything to protect us from the damaging presence of sin in our lives.
- o Read aloud Psalm 38:4, Isaiah 1:16, 18, 2 Corinthians 7:1, and 1 John 1:5-10. How does each of these Scriptures describe sin?
- o What do these descriptions of sin teach us about how sin affects our lives and about how God frees us from sin?

10. When we look at Jesus' interaction with the woman caught in adultery, we don't find even a hint of condemnation. What we do find is an offer to change, an offer at a life that won't keep damaging her, an offer to no longer be branded by her past. Jesus didn't want her to be known for the rest of her life as the woman caught in adultery. He wanted to free her from the condemnation and for a grace-filled future.
- o Describe Jesus' tone with the woman. What does this tell us about his character?
- o What does this story tell us about Jesus' power to rewrite a story?

Deeper Conversation (10-15 minutes)

In advance, write the following on a board or chart. Divide into smaller groups of two or three for deeper conversation.

- Who are some of the "anonymous" people in your life, and how might you help them to feel seen and known?

Closing Prayer (3 minutes)

Close the session by taking personal prayer requests from group members and leading the group in prayer. After giving thanks for all that God has taught you through this study, encourage those in the group to participate in the Closing Prayer by praying aloud for one another and the requests given. Remind participants to continue praying for one another in the weeks to come.

CPSIA information can be obtained
at www.ICGtesting.com
Printed in the USA
LVOW13s0350210217
524865LV00001B/3/P

9 781501 834455